SANTORINI

SUN and LAVA

**MYTHOLOGY - ARCHAEOLOGY
HISTORY**

and

TOURIST GUIDE

ATHENS

ISBN 960-7310-29-2

COPYRIGHT: I. MATHIOULAKIS & Co
ADDRESS: ANDROMEDAS 1 VYRONAS 162 31
                TEL. 7661351 - 7227229
                ATHENS - GREECE
TRANSLATOR: 1 part: ANTONIS POLYCHRONIADIS
                2 part: NANNO MARINATOS

INDEX

SANTORINI

The small but beautiful island of Santorini is located at the south end of the island complex of the Cyclades.

Its first name was "Strongyli" ("Round"). Later it was called "Kalliste" ("Most Beautiful"), and finally Thera. It was named in honor of Theras, son of Autesion (A Theban hero and descendant of Kadmus).

Theras was a regent of Sparta and the guardian of his twin nephews, Proklos and Eurysthenes. After his nephews reached adulthood and assumed the throne, Theras left Sparta, taking with him a group of nobles from Orchomenos, and settled in Kalliste, which was thus named Thera.

The name Santorini is a much more recent one. It comes from the Church of the island, which honored **St. Irene** called **"Aghia Irini"** by the Greeks and **"Santa Rini"** by foreign sailors.

This name became established with the linguistic types **"Santo-Rini"** and **Santorini**.

Many legends and traditions are connected to the existence of this unique island of the Cyclades. It has been ascertained that its present geographical shape and its geological composition -with the exception of Mt. Profitis Ilias- are the result of the action of the local volcanoes.

Santorini is different from the other islands of the Cyclades: it is an island built from the thick lava of the volcano, which rose from the molten core of the earth. Its reddish-black bulk, with the unscalable cliffs, the huge masses of rock, and the hard, impressive colours, are all the products of the volcano's action.

The contrast of the deep blue of the sea with the red, brown, and black colours of the land create a wild, imposing natural beauty not found elsewhere.

Santorini's landscape, together with the colours of the

land and the sea, the rich light, and the depth and clarity of the horizon, create an unforgetable totality, whose charm sweeps away the terror of the nightmarish birth of the island, underlines its dazzling presence, and assures it of winning the first place in the contest of Greek island beauty.

Today, Santorini is no longer the small volcanic island of the Greek archipelago. It is a central island, known all over the world, ready and hospitable to everyone who loves and wants to share its wild natural beauty and be seduced by its light and the clarity of its horizon. Moreover, one can let his imagination travel to the past, to the frightful birth of the island, to feel the insignificance of Man as opposed to the forces of nature, and to follow the ancient inhabitants of the island as they fled the dreadful natural phenomena.

Santorini, however, does not dazzle the visitor solely with the grandeur of a geological phenomenon: it also offers the magic of Atlantis, which legends and the works of Plato identify as this island.

Santorini's incomparable sight cannot leave any visitor unmoved.

TRANSPORT-CONNECTION BY SHIP

The distance between Santorini and Piraeus is about 128 nautical miles. The voyage takes between 10 and 15 hours, as the ships also pass by other islands of the Cyclades.

The ship connection between the island and Piraeus is frequent, and in the summer several ships depart daily from Piraeus to Santorini and vice-versa. There are also frequent connec-

The cable railroad

tions between Santorini and the other Cycladic islands, as well as with Rhodes and Heraclion (Crete).

A local boat connects Santorini with the neighbouring islands.

CONNECTION BY AIR

Several daily flights connect the center (Athens) with Santorini. The flight is short and without delays. There is also an air connection with Heraclion (Crete), Mykonos, and Rhodes.

AREA-POPULATION

Santorini, as it is today, has an area of 76 square kilometers and a population of about 7.000 inhabitants. Its shores are 70 km. long. It consists of the main island, **THERA,** which is shaped like a horseshoe, a smaller one, **Therasia,** located N.W. of the main island, and an even smaller island, **Aspronisi** (White Island), which is S.W. of the opening of the horseshoe, towards the Aegean.

Besides these three islands, there are two more in the aquatic area which is the **caldera** of the volcano; they rise like volcanic cones from its center and they are **PALEA KAMENI** ("Old Burnt Island") and **NEA KAMENI** ("New Burnt Island"),

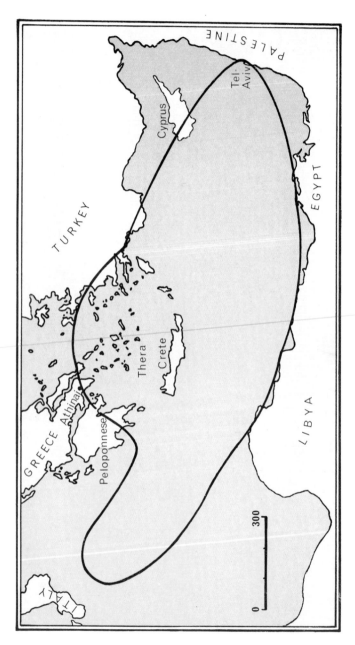

Drawing of the Mediterranean which shows us the extent of the volcano's eruption on 1500 B.C.

12

where the latest crater of the volcano is located.

The length of Santorini, from its most norhern end, Cape Mavropetra, till its southernmost end, Cape Exomytis, reaches 18 km. Its width varies from 2 to 6 km.

MOUNTAINS

The biggest mountain of the island, **Mesa Vouno,** lies S.W. Its highest peak, **Profitis Ilias,** is 550 meters high. To the south lies **Gavrilos,** and to the north **Megalo Vouno,** 350 meters high, and **Mikros Profitis Ilias,** 340 meters high.

CAPES-BAYS

Starting from the northern end of the island, from Cape **Mavropetra,** and sailing along the coasts of Santorini, with an E.-N.E. direction at first and then N.E., N., and N.W., we meet the Capes **Kolumbo, Bourboulo, Kamari, Aghios Georgios, Mesa Vouno,** and **Exomytis.** Cape Exomytis is at the most southern part of the island. From this point, continuing W., we pass by

Kato Fira; the church of Aghios Minas in the background

the Capes **Mavro** and **Akrotiri**. By passing this cape, we enter the caldera. Continuing W., we meet the bays **Athinio** and **Kato Fira**, and the Capes **Skaros** and **Tourlos**. Also the bays **Mouzaki** and **Oia**.

WATER SUPPLIES

Santorini is almost dry. There are very few springs on the island, and even these do not give much water. In the foothills of Mt. Profitis Ilias there is a spring, although it does not give much water. Another one, called **Vryssakia,** is east of the mountain, while a third one is in the west part of the island, near Athinio Bay, in the region called Aghios Ioannis.

For their daily needs, the inhabitants use rainwater, which is collected in special cisterns during the winter. Every house has its own cistern. Today, the island is also supplied with water by water-carrying ships.

HOT SPRINGS

There are four hot, metallic springs on the island. In the Megalohori district the hot spring is known with three names: Atherma, Thermi, and Christ's spring. A second hot spring, Plaka, is in the same district. Kokkina Nera is in the district of the same name, and, finally, Anavrytos spring is in the Emporio village area, in the S. end of the island, near Vlychada.

CLIMATE

Santorini has a typical Aegean island climate. It has a cool summer and a mild winter. It rains often during the winter, but rarely -or not at all- during the summer. Snow may fall ocasionally, but it melts almost immediately.

PRODUCTS

Santorini's fertile volcanic soil, cultivated by its industrious inhabitants, has made the island well known all over Greece for its excellent produce.

Its wines are celebrated. After all, most of the vegetation of the island is grapevines. Also famous is its "fava", a legume smaller than a pea, which looks like a lentil. Its tomatoes are very tasty, too. They are small, the size of a walnut, because of the lack of water. From these tiny tomatoes the famous tomato paste of Santorini is made, which the local people call **"bertes"**. Little produce is grown. Some barley, which is used as animal feed, and even less wheat. A kind of cheese, **"chloro"**, is made from goat milk. It is a tasty cheese. The home-made sausages are very tasty, too. A few animals are bred on the island: some goats, sheep, pigs, and poultry. The production of meat is not sufficient for the present needs of the island.

Finally, Santorini exports the famous **"Theran Earth"** (pumice stone), the sole mineral of the island. Being an island, seafood is not absent, although it is not exported but consumed locally by Santorini's inhabitants and visitors.

One of the beautiful bell-towers of Santorini.

ARCHAEOLOGY

The eastern basin of the Mediterranean took its present aspect during the Pleistocene period.

The area's great geological upheavals had as a result the disappearance of the great mass of land which existed in the place of the contemporary Aegean archipelago. The great number of islands in the eastern Aegean is all that remains from that land which disappeared under the waters of the sea.

In that period, before the volcano begun its action, there was a small rocky island in the place of today's Santorini. A remainder of that non-volcanic island is Mt. Profitis Ilias and its foothills. Deep geological fissures rent asunder the land of the small rocky island and the sea-bottom near it. The red-hot material of the volcanic source found a passage through the fissures of the sea-bottom. The red-hot lava of the volcano formed the first craters. The huge masses of lava which rose to the surface covered a large part of the original island and extended the land, forming a new island, taller and larger than the original island. The height of the new island is estimated to have been 600 to a 1000 meters. The new isle, formed by volcanic matter, had the shape of a trunkated cone. The base of the cone was shaped roughly like a circle, and the round shape of the new volcanic island was responsible for its new name, **"Strongyli"** (Round). With the passing of the centuries, flora and fauna appeared on the dry lava. We cannot claim with any certainty whether the flora and fauna attracted the first men there or was it man who brought the plants and animals to the island.

What is certain, however, is that the island has been inhabited since the neolithic age, as the arhcaeological discoveries indicate. These discoveries, though, are not sufficient to give palaeontologists the elements they need to describe the way of life of these early inhabitants of the area. Later discoveries do give a more complete picture of the society of Thera's prehistoric inhabitants.

The prehistoric inhabitants of the island had developed notable agriculture. They cultivated grapevines, cereals, and fruit trees. Their society was rich and they lived in comfort, as the archaeological discoveries make plain. They did not confine themselves to agriculture, animal breeding, and fishing, but also developed a notable art culture.

The prehistoric inhabitant of Thera has been shown to be a creator of high inspiration and efficiency. Describing the life of the inhabitants of the island, as it was being uncovered, the Greek historian K. Paparigopoulos writes: "These people were wise builders and expert potters, building their houses with hewn stone to prevent the destructive results of the earthquakes. They placed wooden joints between the walls, used the potter's wheel, and made vases with original shapes and beautiful decorations. They wove, fished with nets, and most of their tools were made from hewn stone or obsidian. Finally, they knew gold, silver, copper, tin, and bronze -

Neoclassical architecture at Santorini

and how to use them". Even the art of shipbuilding wasn't unknown to the Therans. They had commercial ties not only with the neighbouring islands but with most powers of the eastern Mediterranean.

Agriculture, animal breeding, fishing, shipping, and commerce were the source of riches of the prehistoric people of Thera. This wondrous civilization, which flowered on a piece of earth born from the destructive fury of Enceladus -and which lived under its constant threat- was stopped and destroyed by the terrible eruption of the volcano in the middle of the 2nd millenium B.C.

It is almost certain that a strong earthquake must have preceded the eruption of the vol-

Twilight at Fira; the villages Mesaria and Pyrgos are discernible in the background

cano. The destruction caused by this most terrible of all known volcanic eruptions in the world took tremendous proportions. The central part of the island blew up and sunk, forming a huge concavity, in both surface area and depth, which was filled by the sea. The scientific name for this concavity is **"caldera"**. Santorini's caldera, together with Lake Oregon, are the largest in the world. The present geographical shape of the island is the direct result of that dreadful explosion.'

When the elements of nature quieted and calm was restored, the islands Thera, Therasia, and Aspronisi were all that had been left above the waters, enclosing the caldera like a wreath. At the same time in which the volcano's explosion changed the face of Thera, another catastrophe was occuring in Crete. The wondrous Minoan civilization was being totally destroyed. The archaeologists spoke about some

The bay ("yalos")

Picturesque lanes at Santorini

military invasion. No one had made the connection between the destruction of Thera and the destruction of Crete. The connection between the biblical catastrophe of Thera and the destruction of Minoan civilization in Crete was first made by the archaeologist Professor Spyros Marinatos. The theory of the wise professor was greeted with scepticism, reservation, and bellicosity.

Archaeological research, though, soon proved that the pioneering researcher was correct. Today we have solid proof which justifies Spyros Marinatos. Before Professor Marinatos had formulated his theory about the simultaneous ruin of Thera and Crete, he had studied other similar volcanic eruptions. The professor, in order to be able to prove as well as ascertain the extent of the catastrophic eruption of Thera's volcano on 1500 B.C., compared it to the eruption of Krakatoa on 1877 A.D. in the Suva Straits, which lie near Java and Sumatra in the Indian Ocean.

The archaeologists' pick has kept bringing to the surface, from under great masses of lava and pumice, towns, cemeteries, inscriptions, pottery, and statuettes since the end of the 19th century.

The fury of the volcano left the previously rich island silent and desolated. Thousands of tons of lava and ash covered its rich towns and villages. Centuries passed. The reddish-black soil of the island lay undisturbed by farmers' hands. No shepherds let their sheep graze in its small valleys, and no primitive boats of some brave seamen approached its rocky shores. The desolation and silence would be broken at some point. Somebody brave enough would dare to approach the steep shores, to climb the precipitous cliffs, and to become master of the island.

According to Greek mythology, Theras and his companions were the first inhabitants of the island after the catastrophe. The tough Dorian got over the awe caused by the sight of the island and landed on its shores.

We do not know whether Theras was a real person, but it is a fact that, in the beginning of the Ist millenium B.C., Thera was settled by Dorian Greeks.

The obstinate Dorians did not take long to master the in-

Therasia: the harbour

hospitable land of the island. A new civilization flowered in the kingdom of silence and desolation. This civilization lacked the subtlety and sensitivity of the Ionian one. Dorian civilization was austere and onerous, thus reflecting its creators. However, the Dorian artists were not uninfluenced by the Ionians on the neighbouring islands. Elements of the subtlety and sensitivity of the Ionian artists also appear in the creations of the Theran artisans.

The capital of the island during the Historic years was the city of Thera. It was so named in honor of King Theras. The city of Thera was discovered by the German archaeologist Hiller von Gaertringen. It was built in the S.W. part of the island, in a rocky area of Mt. Mesa Vouno. On the pass **Sellada,** which connects Mt. Mesa Vouno with the peak Profitis Ilias, the cemetery of ancient Thera was discovered. The excavations are bringing continuously to the surface tombs of the 7th century B.C. as well as significant pottery and ceramics of a more recent age. Ancient ruins and tombs have been discovered in many other parts of the island, such as Gonia, which lies between Finikia and Cape Kolumbo, also in Cape Skaros and Cape Exomytis.

Even Christian art is represented in Santorini with Early Christian, Byzantine and more recent buildings. An example of Byzantine and Venetian castle-building prowess is Castle Skaros.

On the island of Santorini, archaeological research, taking place with consistency and continuity, keeps bringing to light the wondrous art that developed on the island since the prehistoric years.

RELIGION

The Therans, during the idololatric period, worshipped the twelve fods of ancient Greece. They especially honored the god Apollo, who was considered the particular god of the Doric tribe. The mastery of the Ptolemies of Egypt during the Hellenistic years brought the worship of Egyptian deities to the island. The worship of the dead was also widely practiced on Thera.

The island was christianized at about 300 A.D. Both main Christian docrines, the Eastern Orthodox Church and the Catholic Church coexist in Santorini today.

HISTORY

The history of the appearance of man on the island, according to archaeological discoveries, starts from the Neolithic age.

During the 3rd millenium B.C., the island was inhabited by the Karians, a people originating on the coast of Asia Minor. The creation of the naval state of Minoan Crete affected the fortunes of Thera's inhabitants. It did not take long for the Minoan masters of the sea to assert their power on the Therans, both politically and culturally. During the time of the Minoan influence, a remarkable civilization developed.

This civilization, in all its glory, was brought to light at Akrotiri by the archaeologist's pick of Professor Marinatos. The cultural and economic flowering of the island was violenly interrupted by the eruption of the volcano, which took place at about 1500 B.C.

For 5 centuries, the island

Fira: Ypapantis Str. and Marinatos Str.

View of Fira: Skaros seen in the background

One of the many verandas - terraces which we see at Santorini

remained deserted. Possibly around 1200 B.C. the Phoenicians, a sea people of the eastern Mediterranean, appeared there.

In the beginning of the Ist millenium B.C., near the year 1000 B.C., the island was colonized by Dorian Greeks. It is possible that they came from Sparta and had Theras son of Autesion as their leader. Thera remained one of the many independent states of ancient Greece until the end of the Persian wars, on 478 B.C. According to Herodotus, the kingdom of Thera was made up by seven municipalities. The Therans, being Dorian, kept good relations with the Dorian cities of the greater Greek region, and kept the manners and customs of their tribe. It was impossible, though, for them not to be somehow influenced by the Ionians, the other great Greek tribe. The people of Thera, following the example of most Greek cities, on 630 B.C., when Grinnos was king of the island, established a colony on the shores of North Africa, called Cyrene. The leader of the colonists was named Vattos.

With the end of the Persian wars, the naval state of Athens emerged as the strongest in the greater Greek region. The mastery of the Athenian democracy over the Greek islands was complete. The dominant position among the states of Greece which Athens gained by virtue of her strong navy, was called the "alliance" by the Athenians. This alliance is known historically as the First Athenian Alliance, centered originally on Delos, the holy island of the Cyclades. At first, the city-states were enlisted in the alliance as equal "allies". Later, the seat of the alliance was moved to Athens. The move of the seat of the alliance to Athens was the beginning of the repeal of equality among the allies. Steadily the weaker members of the alliance lost their meagre independence and became politically

Loyal friend at Santorini

dependent on Athens. Thera's passing into Athenian dependency occured on 430 B.C.

The Athenians remained lords of Thera until the end of their war with the Spartans. The military defeat of Athens on 404 B.C. (The civil war of the Greeks, known as the Peloponnesian War, lasted from 427 B.C. till 404 B.C.) meant independence for the island.

Athens required a quarter of a century to overcome the consequences of her military defeat. The Athenian triremes reappeared off the island on 378 B.C. to bring it again under the dominion of the reorganized Athenian Alliance. This is the period of the Second Athenian Alliance, which was much inferior in brilliance and power to the First Alliance. The second period of Thera's dependence from Athens ended with the appearance of the Macedonian Greeks in Southern Greece.

The dismemberment of Alexander the Great's empire left Thera as a part of the kingdom of the Ptolemies of Egypt. The Ptolemies remained on the island from 275 B.C. till 146 B.C. The kings of Egypt took military advantage of the island's geographical position. On the south coast of the island the Ptolemies founded Elefsina, a

large naval base which safeguarded the northern frontiers of their state.

The military presence of the Ptolemies on the island was ended by the Roman occupation of Greece on 146 B.C. Thera was occupied by the Romans and enrolled to the Roman prefecture of Asia. Thera, being only an insignificant island in the bound-

The picturesque village of Phira.

less Roman Empire, is not mentioned in Roman historical texts. The Byzantine historians, too, mention Thera only a few times. Purely for information, the Byzantine chronicler Ierocles, and Porfyrogennitos later, wrote that Thera belonged administratively to the Aegean Theme, which had Samos as its capital (Themes were the political and geographical divisions of the Byzantine Empire; they were governed by generals -or admirals for island themes-, on whom both political and military power was concentrated).

The last Crusade ended with the conquest of Constantinople by the crusaders. The lands of the empire were divided among the noble crusader leaders. The Aegean, with its islands, was given to Venice as a reward for the naval support given to the crusaders. The Venetian democracy charged the noble Marco Sanudo with the responsibility of conquering the Aegean. The Venetian admiral appeared in the Aegean on 1207 A.D. His aim was the imposition of the sovereignty of the democracy of St. Mark on the inhabitants of the islands of the Aegean.

Thera was occupied by Sanudo and immediately ceded to his colleague Jacobo Varocci. The Varocci family settled on the island until 1269 A.D. For a little while Thera was reclaimed by the Byzantines, but the Varocci won it back after a military clash between the Venetians and Andronicos B' Palaeologos. The island was also coveted, however, by Nicholas A' Sanudo, Duke of Naxos. Sanudo managed to drive away the Varocci on 1335 A.D. and add Thera to the Dukedom of Naxos. The addition of the island to the Dukedom of Naxos cost the Duke a significant amount of money. The island's adventures do not end, though, with its addition to the Dukedom of Naxos. The Venetian masters of the area, behaving like genuine overlords, sold it, gave it away, or ceded it as dowry. Thus, Duke John Crispi, in the beginning of the 15th century, granted Thera to his brother Marco Crispi, lord of neighbouring Ios. It was given as dowry on 1480 A.D. to the lords Pisani. Thera remained a feud of the Pisani until 1537 A.D., when the Turkish admiral Chairedin Barbarossa established the rule of the Turkish Sultan.

The years of the Venetian presence on the island were characterized by vigorous pirati-

House at Santorini

Vine cultivation: the strange rolling in the shape of a basket is for the protection of the vineyard by strong winds

cal action, which impoverished the inhabitants of the island. Besides the ravages of the pirates, the population had to face the bad administration and the greed of the nobles. The administration of the Dukes was characterized by the poverty and unhappiness of their people. The era of the Pisani was an exception, as an effort to develop the island economically took place at that time. The Pisani period was an economic oasis in a desert of poverty and misfortune. The occupation of Thera by Barbarossa did not bring the Turkish administration on the island immediately. The Turkish Sultan granted Thera to a friend of his, the Spanish adventurer Joseph Nasi. The Ottoman administration was established officially on the island on 1579 A.D.

The Greek Revolution of 1821 A.D. was proclaimed on Thera by Evangelos Mazarakis, an authorized deputy of the revolutionaries on mainland Greece. Thera joined the newly founded Greek state under the Protocol of London (1830).

PLATONIC ATLANTIS/VOLCANIC ERUPTION OF 1500 B.C.

The story of the lost continent of Atlantis moves between the spheres of mythos and reality. Mythology and reality are inseparably tied together. Their separation will solve a mystery which has occupied researchers and authors since the time of Plato. It will deprive, though, all the rest of us, who are neither researchers nor authors, of the beloved and charming magic engendered by this well-known myth.

Archaeologists, historians, and researchers of every kind may someday have the satisfaction of separating myth from history, of solving the mystery of the continent with the wondrous civilization which was lost under the waves because the unbounded egoism of its people caused the anger and the punishment of the gods.

The charming myth of Atlantis passes from the sphere of fantasy to the sphere of reality in the Dialogues of Plato, "Timaeus" and "Critias". It was a large and marvellous country, sovereign of islands and parts of the mainland. The state of Atlantis was a

The wild beauty of the landscape

kingdom of two islands, **Meizon** (Greater) and **Elasson** (Lesser) island. The superiority of the state was cultural rather than military. The kingdom was composed by ten cities. Plato, in "Critias", describes two of these cities, **Metropolis** and **Vasiliki Politeia** (King's City). From Plato's description of the islands we draw the conclusion that Metropolis was the island Strongyli, which today is Santorini, and that Vasiliki Politeia was Crete.

The research of the archaeologists Spyros Marinatos and Nikos Platon assured both scientists that the mythical Atlantis was Santorini, according to Marinatos, while Platon identified it with Minoan Crete. Both accept that Atlantis was destroyed by the volcanic eruption of 1500 B.C. Also, the geologist Professor Angelos Galanopoulos writes: "For those who know, even if superficially, the great civilizations of the Bronze Age, Platonic Atlantis is projected as a civilization of that era". Afterwards he mentions the earthquake and the great eruption of the volcano on 1500 B.C., comparing it to the eruption of Krakatoa. In the Krakatoa eruption, 2/3 of the island collapsed, specifically 33,52 kilometers to a depth of 200-300 meters.

In Santorini, 83,52km. were submerged to a depth of 300-400 m. The sudden movement of so great masses of water (837,5 trillion cubic meters of water at Krakatoa, 41875 trillion c.m. of water at Strongyli/Santorini) caused great tidal waves. The initial height of the "Tsunami" wave at Krakatoa was 100 meters. At Strongyli, the initial height of the Tsunami was 210 meters (**TSUNAMI** is the scientific name for the tidal wave caused by a volcanic eruption), and when it reached Crete its height exceeded 70 meters. If the eruption of the Santorini volcano was equivalent to that of Krakatoa, the sound of the explosion would have been heard to the Scandinavian peninsula.

Professor Spyros Marinatos wrote about this terrible eruption and its consequences: "Thera, a volcanic island, had in the past the round shape usual to such islands. For many centuries, the volcano had been sleeping. Flourishing settlements were built on the island, probably in part as a Minoan colony, because they had houses ornamented with frescoes, decorated pottery and remarkable utensils of every kind.

At some point the volcano erupted. In the beginning it emitted great amounts of pumice

Night at Fira

and volcanic ash which covered the island under a layer 30 meters deep. The sea around the island was covered by pumice in an area of thousands of meters. The settlements of the island were buried under this layer. Finally, in a paroxysm, the volcano blew up and sank the whole central and western part of the island, forming today's caldera, the largest of its kind. Only the eastern, sickle-shaped, part of the previously round island remained above the waves, while from the western part, which was sunk, two shoals-rather than is-lands- remained, Therasia and Aspronisi.

Volcanoes are divided into families. A sister volcano to Thera is Krakatoa, in the Indian Ocean, the great eruption of which took place on 1887. Geologists tell us that the same things happened to Thera as to Krakatoa. Thus we have an un-usual vessel to recreate the results of the eruption of Thera. The 1887 eruption caused ter-rible damage around Krakatoa. Day became night in a radious of 150 km. or more. The terrible sounds of the explosions destroyed houses, and volcanic ash was cast hundreds of kilometers away from the point of the eruption. Because of the electrical charge of the atmosphere, lightning hit many buildings, while the sound waves caused by the noise of the explosion travelled round the globe repeatedly. The greatest destruction, though, was caused by a series of waves of up to 15 meters height, which, with deadly speed, crashed on the neighbouring inlands of Sumatra and Java. Whole towns (Teloek-Betoeng) disappeared under the fury of the waves, as well as blocks of stone, steam engines, and railway tracks. A steamship was raised high by the waves, and after it was carried over the town, it was deposited intact several kilometers inland, in a forest. At the same moment -and this is the strange thing- fires burst in Teloek-Betoeng. More than 36.000 people were lost during this dreadful calamity. The eruption of Thera was four times stronger than that of Krakatoa. The distance between Thera and Crete is 60 miles, which is shorter than the distance between Krakatoa and Teloek-Betoeng. Moreover, the sea is incomparably deeper near Thera than it is in Krakatoa, while the speed of the waves grows with a certain mathematical formula as the depth of the sea is increasing. In a time span that was less than an hour, the waves, tall as mountains, reached with ruinous speed the northern shores of Crete. All coastal settlements, which were flourishing until then, were carried away in a matter of minutes, while day, if the final explosion took place in the daytime, became night" (Marinatos-Hirmer: Crete and Minoan Greece).

For about 1500 years the volcano remained dormant. The ash and pumice which covered the island erased its previous existence from human memory. A civilization whose glory is reflected in the city of Akrotiri passed into the sphere of legend.

The volcano from Fira

THE VOLCANIC ERUPTIONS
AFTER 1500 B.C.

After the destruction of the island and the formation of the caldera the volcano remained dormant for about 1500 years. It took that many years for the conditions which were necesarry for the seemingly quiet volcano to act again to be recreated. After the passing of the years of peace, the volcano became energetic again under the sea, in the center of the caldera. The eruptions which took place during the historic years did not have the intensity of the 1500 B.C. eruption, nor did they cause catastrophes. Certain of them, though, were truly terrible. The emerging white-hot materials created new domes which emerged as islands on the surface of the sea.

The first eruption of the volcano after the one of 1500 B.C. took place at 197 B.C. The island Palea Kameni was formed by the lava of this eruption.

There is not much information about the eruptions of 19 A.D. and 146 A.D. They are just mentioned by the chroniclers.

The Byzantine chronicler Kedrinos refers to the eruption of 726 A.D. This eruption formed an islet which was joined to the already existing Palea Kameni.

A disagreement exists on whether the eruption which formed Nea Kameni island took place on 1570 or 1573 A.D. The eruption of May, 1707, has been described by a Catholic priest. The clergyman, in his chronicle, gives a vivid impression of the fury of the elements, as well as of the panic that the anger of Enceladus caused to the population. The good clergyman gives an elegant description of the emergence of the new shoal from the bottom of the sea. Brave Santorinians visited it only ten days after its first appearance. The panic and the fear of the eruptions, the smoke, the fire, the ashes, the view of the new land, the wild sea, and the earthquakes, was soon replaced by familiarity. From the end of August, all the above, which had been panicking the people of Thera, had become outdated. The prayers and the liturgies stopped, and only curiosity about what the next day would bring remained. Little by little the volcano settled down, and, at last, after five years (1712) quieted for about 155 years.

The eruption which took place on 20/2/1866 was very large. For four years, the volcano did not quiet. During this volcanic action the domes Georgios and Afroeresa were formed.

Two of the numerous picturesque churches of the island.

Later they were both joined to Nea Kameni.

The 20th century is not a century of quiet for the volcano. On 1925 (II August-31 May 1926) the volcano resumed its activity. The result of this activity was the formation of the dome of Dafni, which later joined the Georgios dome. Both domes together, formed, in their final phase, a single island with Nea Kameni.

A small-scale eruption was that of January-March (23/1-17/3) 1928. The volcanic activity of this period formed the dome Nautilos on the lava of Dafni. A new eruption occured on August, 1939. This time the volcano remained active for two years. The volcano quieted down finally on July, 1941. During the two year period that the volcano was active, seven new domes appeared. The last activity of the subterranean giant occured during January 1950. This weak action ended on 2/2/50 and created one dome. All the domes which were formed during the 1925-50 period have joined in a single totality known with the name Neai Kamene (New Burnt Islands). On 1956 strong earthquakes shook the island of Santorini, but the expected eruption failed to take place. The earthquakes caused the death of 57 people and material damage as well. Hot vapours and sulphurous gases are coming out continuously from the crater of the volcano. A visit to the volcano can be made by boat. The depth in which the source of magma that feeds the volcano is located is estimated to be 1000 meters under the surface of the sea.

VISITING SANTORINI

The official name of the island is Thera, but the name Santorini has prevailed.

The visitor of the island lives a rare experience when the ship, sailing slowly, passes and leaves Aspronisi behind, and enters the deep blue waters of the **caldera.**

Tall reddish-back cliffs and granite rocks, of imposing appearance, frighten and cause awe as they rise vertically from the surface of the sea. Barely seen is the road which, like a snake, unfolds on the cliff and joins the town with the harbour.

The deep blue colour of the sea, the reddish-black of the cliffs, and the smoke that is seen in the background from the crater of Nea Kameni, compose a unique picture of wild beauty. On the edge of the cliff, literally hanging over the sea, a long white ribbon is discernible. It is the town of Fira, the capital of the island and the district of the same name. As the ship approaches, the beaches of black sand begin to be discernible, the red-black stones of the coasts, the cable railway, and the road which leads from the coast to the top of the cliff, where the white town spreads. Narrow streets which seem to be -but are not- cul-de-sacs, bring the visitor to some beautiful crossroads on a roof, which is not only a roof but the courtyard of the house above, or even a road, or bring you in front of the door of some picturesque Santorinian house.

If you happen to be in Oia, the other big village of the island, one of these streets may bring you, where it ends, to the edge of the cliff. If you are lucky and evening approaches, and the sun is getting ready to dive into the vastness of the sea, don't turn back, do not commit the crime of turning your back to it. Stay, even if you are not a romantic. If you leave, it will be your loss; so stay and enjoy one of the most beautiful sunsets that your eyes may ever see.

The beaches of Santorini, if we compare them with the beaches of the other Cyclades,

The town of Fira built on the edge of the cliff

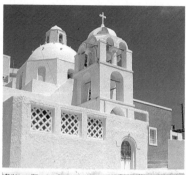

One of the many churches of the island

have their own beauty, that makes them special. The black sand, the black gravel, and the pumice-stone give the beaches of the island their own colour.

In the south and east, in contrast to the awesome landscape of the west part of the island, lie shores many kilometers long, with wide sandy beaches, some organized and some free, which offer the visitor the joys of sun and sea. The means of transportation in the interior of the island are extremely good. A dense road network joins the villages, the archaeological sites, and the beaches of the island with the town of Fira. Buses leave Fira on a regular time-table, about every half-hour, for the villages and archaeological sites. There are taxis not only in Fira but in all large villages of the island. Moreover, there are boats for hire, either speedboats or rowboats.

The possibilities for recreation are not limited. There is great choice in the kind of entertainment offered on the island, from discos to local folk music and dances. You still may, if you like, attend the local fairs, which honor the memory of various Saints. Some take place in the summer, as, for example, the fair of Aghios Ioannis on 24/7 at Monolithos, or the Stavros fair, or the Profitis Ilias fair on 20/7, or the Panaghia fair on August 15, etc.

The possibilities of one occupying himself with sports other than swimming or fishing, with a boat you own or rent, are limited. Only in Kamari you may find places which rent surfboards. There is only one tennis-court on the whole island, in the Karterados area.

If you want to buy the famous Santorinian fava, be careful and don't buy it from a store; there is great possibility of it being imported. You should buy it directly from a producer. Also, if you buy wine, prefer bottled wine, or, again, buy it from a producer.

For any emergency that may

occur, the visitor should refer to the Police in Fira, or to the Port Authority, also in Fira.

In the summer season, before one arrives on the island, he should have made certain he has a place to stay. Otherwise, it is very probable that he will not be able to find shelter. In such cases, he should ask the Police or the Port Autority for help.

In cases of sickness or accident, there is a Health Station in Fira, as well as country doctors in Oia, Emporio, Pyrgos and Therasia.

There is a Post Office, an office of O.T.E. (Greek telephone and telegraph company), and an office of E.O.T. (National Tourist Organization of Greece) at Fira. Oia also has offices of E.O.T. and O.T.E. A bank is also located at Fira.

The great number of churches is impressive. The churches and chapels reach the amazing number of 352.

The blue and white colours give a special beauty to the houses of Santorini

FIRA

The town of Fira stands out like a white eagles'-nest, hanging between sea and sky. The climb from the bay to the town can be made on foot for those who want to try their strength, climbing the 600 steps of the road, or with the cable railroad. There also are good-natured donkeys, who offer their backs to those who want to enjoy the experience of donkey-riding. Their pack-saddles are decorated with blankets of many colours, "kilimia", and the coloured beads on their harnesses give a unique and joyful colour, which is still maintained on an island which is fighting to keep its local colour and its folk personality.

The capital of the island was moved to Fira from Pyrgos Kallistis in the beginning of the 19th century. Now Fira is a growing town with a population of about 1500 people, which lives in the present but tries to retain the local traditions of the past.

In the summer, a loud and good-natured crowd of people strolls, carefree, on the roads which are parallel to the cliff and the small streets that cross them.

A view of the town of Fira

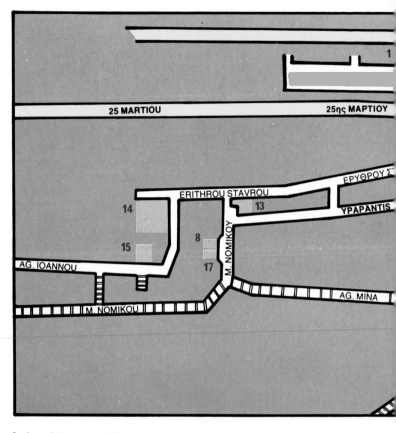

A plan of the town of Fira

KEY TO MAP OF TOWN OF SANTORINI

1. Police
2. Port-office
3. Telecommunications (O.T.E.)
4. Olympic Airways offices
5. Post office
6. Bank
7. Customhouse
8. Town Hall
9. Museum

10. Bus station
11. Taxi station
12. St. Ioannis
13. Museum
14. Catholic Monastery
15. Catholic church
16. Cathedral
17. Teleferik
18. Hospital

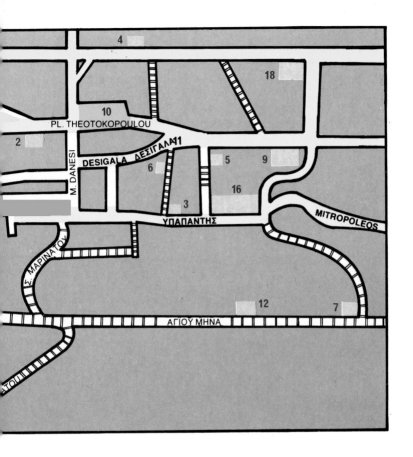

The central part of the town, the market, is here. Numerous shops offer a great variety of merchandice, satisfying even the most demanding customers. Also, the offered merchandice, from the cheapest (cotton shirts and blouses) to the most expensive (furs and jewelry) give it a particular accent which is quite interesting to the visitor. The visit

to the picturesque market of Fira is a pleasant walk. Small houses, dug in the land, one- or two-storied, have a view of either the sea or the land. Lit and crowded against each other, as they are, on the top of the cliff, they seem to be wanting to support each other, so they can reach outward, over the abyss. Terraces of houses which are not terraces but balconies or passages, vaults and archways, and small, white, decorated facades. Straight lines are unknown, everything is in curves, giving a unique architectural characteristic to the houses of Fira which are sunk inside the earth. "Skafta" (dug) as the locals call them, they are built from stone and the earth of the island.

Do not wonder if, when passing through the door of a building which is, at first glance, one-storied, you walk many steps down and yet do not end in some dank and dark basement, but, when you open your window, you see the sea reflecting the sun, although you have descended two or three storeys inside the earth.

At Fira, buildings do not have height, they have depth.

The **ARCHAEOLOGICAL MUSEUM** of the town of Fira features collections from the excavations of Mesa Vouno, where Ancient Thera and the Sellada cemetery are, from Akrotiri, and various utensils from other areas.

Amphoras, pottery, earthen casks, marble Kouroi, female statuettes, coins, etc. are sheltered in the halls of the museum. These collections cover a long period, which starts in the third millennium B.C. and ends in the Roman years.

CHURCHES Fira is the seat for both an Orthodox and a Catholic bishop. The Metropolitan church of Ypapanti was built on 1827 by Marko Belonias, and that is why it is called "Panaghia of Belonia". The original building was destroyed by the earthquakes of 1956 (July 9). In its place a new church, Metamorphosis, was built. There also are the Catholic church and the Convent of the Dominican Order.

The visit to the old mansions and houses of the town is interesting. Among the mansions, Gyzi's, an authentic building of the Venetian years, stands out. Today it belongs to the Catholic church of the island. It has been restored and is used for various cultural meetings. The building houses an impressive collection of antiques, furniture, engravings, and other art objects from centuries past.

FIROSTEFANI It's a small, elongated village, very near Fira, which seems more like a neighborhood of Fira than a separate village. Among the sights of the village are the churches of Ag-

MAP OF SANTORINI

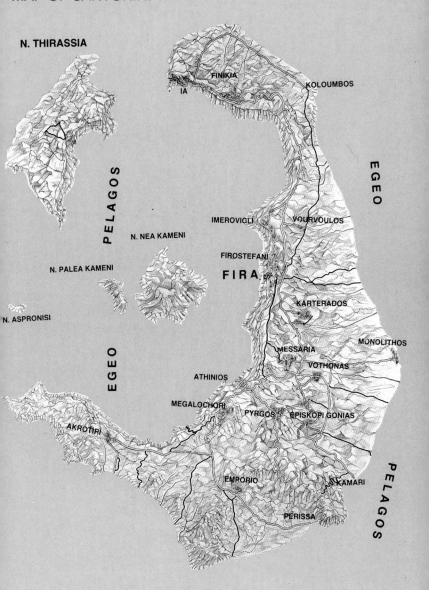

N. THIRASSIA

PELAGOS

N. NEA KAMENI

N. PALEA KAMENI

N. ASPRONISI

EGEO

IA

FINIKIA

KOLOUMBOS

EGEO

IMEROVIGLI

VOURVOULOS

FIROSTEFANI

FIRA

KARTERADOS

MONOLITHOS

MESSARIA

VOTHONAS

ATHINIOS

MEGALOCHORI

PYRGOS

EPISKOPI GONIAS

AKROTIRI

EMPORIO

KAMARI

PERISSA

PELAGOS

hios Minas and Aghios Georgios.

The view of the volcano and the caldera are panoramic. The most picturesque part of the village is its rebuilt part, which is next to the edge of the cliff. The Catholic church is also interesting. The Catholic's area, the "Frangika", is located between Fira and Firostefani. The convents of the Dominicans and the Sisters of Mercy are there. Also, the Lazarists founded there the Greco-French school of St. Joseph.

IMEROVIGLI OR MEROVIGLI, as the locals call it, is very near, about 1km. N.W. of the village of Firostefani. Its location near the edge of the cliff, its name, of the day-Vigla, as well as the time when it was built, show that during the years of the pirates' attacks it had been a daily observatory. The Viglator -guard- watched the sea, and, if pirates appeared, apprised the population of the approaching danger. Most old buildings are ruined. The church of Panaghia Malteza is interesting. It is called Malteza (Maltese) because the icon of the Virgin was found on the port of Malta by a Santorinian captain and carried to Imerovigli, where the captain built a church for it.

THE CONVENT OF ST. NICHOLAS is the oldest convent of the island. It was built in its present position on 1815-20. Originally, the convent had been built in inaccesible Skaros, but the nuns moved it from the ruined castle of Skaros to its present position. The Gyzis family had a private temple in impassable Skaros, dedicated to the memory of St. Nicholas. On 1651, the family got permission from the Bishop to convert the small church to a convent. The girls of the Gyzis family became the first nuns. The convent became property of the Greek state on 1849.

In the center of the convent's courtyard, there is the handsome triune church of St. Nicholas. The 32 cells of the nuns are in the buildings around the church. The attention of the visitor is drawn to the temple screen and the old icons.

SKAROS Majestic Skaros rises perpendicularly to the coast, on the most northern end of the area. The medieval capital of Santorini was built in an inaccesible and unapproachable area. The castle was built by a Roman noble named Scaurus, who was governor of the island when it was possessed by the Romans. The castle, built on top of a steep, dark, and dreadful crag, was one of the five medieval castles of the island, seat of the Venetian Archons and of the Catholic bishops. The remains of the castle and the ruins of the Venetian buildings are discernible. Ancient ruins and graves have been found in the area.

The church of Theoskepasti ("God-covered") is interesting. The church was built by a seaman who believed that he was saved from a great storm with the Virgin's help. Most of the 352 churches of Santorini have been built by seamen whose patron Saint saved them from storms or other great dangers.

VOURVOULOS The village Vourvoulos, the village of the mule-guides of Santorini, is located east of Imerovigli. Most Santorinian mule-guides are descended from this village. In the area Kato Vourvoulos we find the wonderful church of St. Panteleimon.

FOINIKIA Lies about 9km. from Fira. Good roads and regular transportation connect this village with the capital of the island. Foinikia, Oia, and Tholos, with its few houses, are the villages of north Santorini, the Upper

View from Oia

Side, as the locals call it. Foinikia is a representative traditional Santorinian village. Houses built with the traditional ways, harmoniously attached to each other, present a wonderful totality of traditional architecture. A black stone wall rises like a fence near the entrance of the village. In the Gonia region there is an archaeological site.

OIA The distance that separates Oia from Fira is not over 10km. of paved road. The small houses, carved into the rock, the mansions with their stairways and their neoclassical architecture, with white and ochra as their dominant colours, the walls decorated with small stones, the roads paved with flagstones, and the flowers, form a harmonious total of the impressive picture of the village. The village square is a balcony looking at the caldera. The view of the volcano and the infinity of the sea take a different dimension when seen from here. The wealth of the villagers of the last century is exhibited in the Nautical museum of Oia. Oia's inhabitants were sailors, and became rich in the last century by working in the sea. They decorated their village with neoclassical buildings which today bear witness to an age that has passed.

The church of Aghiou Sozontos (Saviour) was built before 1680. The sunset will be not forgotten by those who enjoy it.

BEACHES There are two beaches in the Oia area. The access is difficult though, as they cannot be reached by car. One can only go on foot. If someone wants to go to the **"Armeni"** beach, where the harbour is, he should descend about 300 steps. The road to **"Ammoudi"** beach has about 200 steps. A good road is the one that goes to the huge beach of the **"Baxedes"** area. This area is about 3km. away from Oia. Near the back side of the village is **"Katharos"** beach. There is a country infirmary in Oia.

KOLOUMBOS The other volcano of Santorini, the crater of which is underwater. Its distance from Fira is about 20km. The volcano's eruption on 1650 A.D. was quite strong. It was accompained by earthquakes, tidal waves, and poisonous gases. Areas near Perissa and Kamari were flooded, and ancient ruins

The harbour. This is where the stepped road starts. It leads to the capital of the island Thera.

One of the many taverns of Santorini

came to the surface when the waters receded. The sound of the explosion was heard at Chios, and the coasts of Asia Minor were covered by a thin layer of ash. The tidal wave reached Crete. The explosion period was called the "Bad Time" by the inhabitants. When peace and quiet were reestablished, the locals built the church of Panaghia tou Kalou ("Virgin of the Good") on the Koloumba site. In the cape area there are images carved on the rocks, They are the so-called "cells". These images, carved on the rocks, are inscriptions with the names of gods and heroes, and are characteristic of Santorini.

BEACHES An extended beach, perfect for enjoying the sea, starts from Cape Kolumbo and continues till Cape Exomytis. As an indication we'll mention the Pori, Kanakari, and Exo Yalou beaches and other areas.

MONOLITHOS This typical village of Santorini is near the island's airport. It lies about 7km. from Fira. An organized beach is in operation there.

KARTERADOS The village is east of Fira, at a distance of less than 2km. The architecture of the village's houses is interesting. The church of Analipsis is worth seeing.

MESARIA The village is about 4km. distant from Fira, to the S.E. This beautiful village of Santorini is surrounded by vineyards and gardens. Mesaria is a production center of the famous Santorinian wine. The village churches of Metamorphosis tou Soteros and Aghia Irini were built between 1680 and 1700.

VOTHONAS A village near Fira. The "dug" houses of the village are interesting, as well as the churches of Aghia Triada, Aghia Anna, and Panaghia, which was built on 1700. The

Fira: the Metropolis

church is "dug" at a height of about 20 meters from the ground, on a raised parapet called "trafos". It was used as a shelter by the people of Vothonas during attacks by pirates. After the people had climbed on the parapet, they pulled the wooden ladder. The twenty meters that separated them from the ground provided ample protection. The church is also known under the name Panaghia i Trypa (Virgin of the Crypt).

KAMARI A modern tourist village, continually evolving. About 10km. distant from Fira in a S.W. direction. A sight of the village is the church of Myrtidiotissa. Many ancient artifacts have been found in the area. Ancient Oia, the port of the ancient capital of Thera, was here. A road connects Kamari with the archaeological site of ancient Thera.

The area has a beach many kilometers long. It is made of black sand and pebbles. The enjoyment of sun and sea has no limits.

EPISKOPI GONIAS In the area of the village Mesa Gonia, which is about 6km. distant from Fira and very near Kamari, Episkopi Gonias, a church dedicated to the Assumption of the Virgin, is located. The church is of the Byzantine style, cross-shaped, with a cupola and ante-temple. It was built in the end of the 11th century, with all expenses paid by the Byzantine emperor Alexios Komnenos. Large tracts of land were given to the church by imperial warrant.

Today, the building we see is altered by additions. Certain examples of Byzantine hagiography of the 11th century have been preserved on the arches of the church. The marble screen of the temple is intact. The church was the seat of the bishop of Thera. After the island was occupied by the Venetians on 1207, the Orthodox bishop was driven out, and the expulsion was followed by the installation of a Catholic bishop. When Santorini was occupied by the Turks on 1537, a new dispute started between Catholics and Orthodox. The long clash between the two docrines caused the intervention of the Patriarch of Constantinople. The Orthodox Patriarch, with the Turkish Sultan concurring, ceded the possession of the temple to the Orthodox, and divided the property of the church equally among the two docrines. The Patriarchal decision of 1614 ended the clash and restored peace among the two Christian communities and the clergy that represented them.

PYRGOS Located 8km. south of the town of Fira. The castle is built on the top of a round hill. The imposing settlement with its white picturesque buildings was the capital of the island till 1800. Tradition says that Pyrgos was one of the settlements of ancient Thera. Ruins of the medieval Venetian castle are preserved in the middle of the village. On top of the hill is the so-called Kasteli, which, with its beautiful view and its formation, is recommended for relaxation. The church of Theotokos, also called Theotokaki, a 10th century building, is also at Pyrgos. The chapel is the oldest medieval building of the area. The churches of the area are many, and all are of some interest, especially those built before 1650, as Aghia Theodosia, Taxiarchis Michael, and other saints of the Orthodox Church. A country infirmary is also there.

PROFITIS ILIAS MONASTERY The monastery of Profitis Ilias is located on the peak of the mountain of the same name, at a height of 550 meters. The monastery's construction was started on 1771 by the monks Joacchim and Gabriel. The two monks, with the permission and the help of the bishop of Thera, Zacharias, managed to obtain the sanction of the Patriarch of Constantinople, Cyril, to build the monastery. So, the newly founded monastery came under the spiri-

Kamari beach

tual protection of the Patriarchate and was titled a "Patriarchal Monastery". The building we see today is larger than the original. The monastery took its present form in the middle of the 19th century, when the King of Greece, Othon, visited Santorini. Othon was charmed by the landscape and urged that the monastery be expanded. The museum of the monastery is rich in ecclesiastical articles of inestimable value. Excepting the holy relics there, there are icons of the 15-18 centuries, gold-adorned vestments, the diamond-adorned mitre of the Patriarch Gregory E', silverbound Scriptures, an iron cross of the 12th century (it is said that

this cross was used by the Crusaders) and wood-carved ecclesiastical masterpieces.

The library of the monastery is impressive. It contains leather-bound books, hand-written Codexes, and various other ecclesiastical documents in many languages, as the five tomes of the New and Old Testament written by a son of Philip B' of Spain in Hebrew, Latin, and Greek. The leather-bound books alone number over 1200. The wood-carved temple screen of the church is impressive, as is the bell of the monastery. The monastery also contains a Folk Museum. This museum exhibits the tools of the various trades that the monks and the people of the island practiced. Complete workshops of the past century, fully equipped, seem to be waiting for the candle-maker, the barrel-builder, the blacksmith and the cobbler to start sweating in front of the bellows or the bench with the leather skins. The private Nomikos collection, which is housed in the Monastery, includes embroidery, woven articles, and porcelain. The spiritual contribution of the monastery was limited, though, and cannot be compared to the activities of other monasteries. The only spiritual institution established by this monastery was some school in Pyrgos.

PERISSA A seaside settlement with a magnificent and interminable beach. The dark sea and the surrounding green make it one of the most beautiful on the island. The rocky bulk of Mesa Vouno, the remainder of ancient Aigiis, rises east of the village.

One of the island's largest churches, if not the largest, Timios Stavros ("Holy Cross") is located in Perissa. On the S.E. coast, not far from the village, is the monastery of Perissa. It is a 19th century building and has a five-domed church. the monastery was built on the ruins of the old church of Aghia Irini, which, it is believed, had given the island its name. But Aghia Irini itself had been built on the ruins of another, older church.

Oia: the harbour from above

ANCIENT THERA The ancient capital of Thera. It is located on the S.W. part of the island, 15km. S.E. from Fira or 10km. S.E. from Kamari, built on a rocky slope of Mesa Vouno, at an elevation of 350 meters. The length of the ancient city (archaeological site) is not more than 800m., while its width approaches 200m. The archaeological site, the way it is shaped now, is an oblong area traversed by a central road and its branches.

The German archaeologist Hiller V. Gaertingen excavated the area during 1895-1903, on his own expense, and brought to light the ancient capital of Thera,

The Metropolis church at Emporio

The great steeple at Empo

the city of the mythical King Theras.

The city of Thera was the center of the island for a whole millenium. The buildings, the temples, the vases, the pottery, and the coins that have been found, record accurately the thousand-year long history of the island, from the age of the Dorians to the age of the Roman Empire.

The choice of location must have not been random. It may be connected to the defensive needs of the inhabitants of the island during the first millenium B.C. This interpretation is supported by the partly preserved strong walls that surrounded the city.

Picturesque chapel on the crossroads going to Pyrgos

A road paved with flagstones led from the capital to its port, ancient Oia (today's Kamari). A visit to the archaeological site may start from Fira, Kamari, or Perissa. The excavations that took place along the road between ancient Thera and Kamari brought to light tombs of the Hellenistic and Palaeochristianic periods, which were hewn into the rock. The various artifacts found there, including clay vases, pottery, and gravestones, are ex-

A steeple at Fira

Traditional chimney

*, The church of
Aghios Nikolaos at
the warm springs
behind the volcano*

*The little port and
the church of Saint
Taxiarchi in Nea
Kameni.*

*The church of
Aghios Nikolaos to
the right of the
ancient city of
Akrotiri*

hibited in the Archaeological Museum of Fira.

If we enter the ancient city from the left side, we see the small Byzantine church of Aghios Stephanos. This small church was built in the place where the palaeochristianic church of the Archangel Michael stood, as a marble inscription on the left wall informs us. Following the ancient road south, we meet the temple of the hero Artemidoros, an admiral of the Ptolemies. Engraved on the rocks are inscriptions, holy animals, the Ptolemaean eagle, the lion of Apollo, and Neptune's dolphins. Above and to the right of the dolphins, the head of Artemidoros is discernible. The symbols of the Dioscuri, Hecate, and Priapos are also distinguishable. Following the road to the edge of the city, we reach the church of Evangelismos tis Theotokou ("Annunciation of the Virgin"). The tomb of some hero is next to the church. From here, following the uphill road, we reach the archaic temple of Apollo Karneios. A temple of the Doric style, without an external collonade, with a court and a room for the priest, a portico, a sanctuary, and two small shrines. An external doorway is preserved. On the walls and rocks a large number of names of gods is discernible, written in the ancient Theran alphabet of the 7th century B.C. Next to the temple there is something resembling a raised court or terrace ("doma"), where the "orcheiseis" (dances) took place when the Dorians honored the god Apollo on his 9 day long festival, the "Karneia". S.E. of the temple we find the Gymnasium of the Epheboi, a building of the 2nd century B.C. Here we also find inscriptions praising the manners and the customs of the Dorians. The holy cavern of Hermes and Heracles is located here. There are the remains of a bath near the west side of the Gymnasium. Following the main road of the city towards its center, we see the remains of private residences right and left. The Agora is located on the center of the city. On its west side we find the Vasiliki Stoa (Royal Portico), a Roman building, very probably of the reign of Augustus. It had an internal collonade of 12 columns which supported the roof of the building, and a separate space for the statues of the imperial family. Next to the portico is a small temple of the Hellenistic period dedicated to the worship of Dionysos. At this temple, during the reign of Augustus, the emperor was worshipped. To the south of the

Agora the ruins of the city's theater, of the Hellenistic period, are preserved. The theater was also used for assemblies. During the reign of Caligula, statues of his mother Agrippina, as Hestia Voulaia,

Ancient Thera.

and of his father Germanicus, as Zeus Voulaios, had been erected there. West of the theater a Hellenistic building with a column-supported court may have been used as a place of assembly for the religious cult of the "Valistes", who worshipped the King.

The temple of Pythios Appolo, which was later converted to a Christian church, is behind the house of the Valistes. Also the temples of the Egyptian deities Isis, Serapis, and Anubis. To the N.W. side of the city are the "barracks" and the "Gymnasium" of the Ptolemies. Among others, private residences, hot baths, and a temple of Ptolemy III have been uncovered.

A little to the north there is an ancient temple which was converted to a Christian church, the Sotiras tou Christou ("Christ

Saviour"). It is also called Christoulaki (Little Christ). Next to the church, in a natural cavern, there are the temples of Demetra and Persephone.

The cemetery of the ancient city is found in the Sellada area, a pass of Mesa Vouno. In the location Plagiades, on the N.E. side of the pass, 7th century B.C. tombs have come to light, with important funeral gifts. Another cemetery has been uncovered on the S.W. side of Mesa Vouno. The excavations, which started on 1895 and are still continuing, keep bringing to the surface artifacts from an age that was considered all but mythological a few years ago.

The fresco of the adorant.

Temenos of Artemidoros.

MEGALOHORI The village is about 9km. distant from Fira. Except for the churches of the Eisodia tis Theotokou and Aghioi Anargyroi, on the road to Emporio we find the church of Aghios Nicolaos Marmaritis. It is called Marmaritis because the whole building is made of marble ("marmaro"). This church was a pagan temple of the Doric style before the 4th century A.D. Its conversion to a Christian church left the original building of the 3rd century A.D. intact.

EMPORIO or NIMPORIO A large village with a population of about 1000 people. It is built almost on the center of the plain, on a point which has a view towards both sides of the island. Small, picturesque streets and old mansions compose the beauty of the old village. It was one of the five areas of the island fortified with a castle during the Venetian years. Vestiges of the medieval castle (Mesana), which was equal to Pyrgos, remain till this day. North of the village, a bulky, square building, "Goulas", is located. It is a strong tower in which the people of the village found shelter and protection from the pirates. Tradition claims that this tower was built by monks from the Monastery of St.

John in Patmos to protect the land and wealth of the monastery. The imposing church of Evangelismos is a modern building, built in the 1980's. To the right of the village, lining the hill, we see the picturesque windmills of Gavrilos.

AKROTIRI A village in the S.W. part of the island, about 12km. distant from Fira. It is built on the most remote part of the island. The excavations in the area brought to light the settlement known as the City of Akrotiri.

It was one of the fortified castles of the island during the medieval years. After Santorini was occupied by the Turks, the strong Venetian castle was torn down. The remains of its towers are easily discernible. The old churches of Aghia Triada and Ypapanti tou Soteros are found in the area. From here, a road leads to the southern part of the island, where Faros is.

ATHINIO BAY The sole harbour of the island. The village has very old domed houses, dug in the volcanic rock, and these are the only sights worth seeing there.

A small beach, covered with pebbles, is good for swimming.

THERASIA Small island opposite Oia. About one hour distant from Santorini. One can visit this small and barren island, with the few inhabitants, with an excursion boat. Its only sight is the wood-carved temple screen in the monastery Koimisis tis Theotokou. The screen was made in Russia and placed in the church on 1872. The coasts of the island are out of the way and the beaches very few. A road with 150 steps leads from the harbour to the village Manola, the largest settlement on the island. Other villages on the island are Potamos and Agrilia. On the south end of the island there is a submarine cave, called Trypiti, that has two entrances. On the north side of the island is the church of Aghia Irini, which lays claim to the honor of having changed Thera's name to Santorini together with Aghia Irini of Perissa.

There is a country infirmary on the island.

The chapel of Aghios Nikolaos adjoined to the rock

PALAIA and NEA KAMENI

The two volcanic islands, where the crater of the volcano is. The visit to the volcano is made by boat. The whole area smells heavily of sulphur, while on many points the stones and earth are hot. The trip and the climb to the crater take about 1 1/2 hours.

Like a white eagle's nest, hanging between sea and sky, the town of Fira stands out.

The medieval castle Goulas at Emporio

AKROTIRI

History of the Excavation

The excavations at Akrotiri began in 1967 by Prof. Sp. Marinatos. He chose to excavate there in the hope of verifying a theory which he had formulated some thirty years ago when he was still a young man at the beginning of his career.

This theory was borne in Crete when Sp. Marinatos was digging a Minoan villa at Amnissos, the harbour-town of Knossos. While excavating, he was struck by the extent of the violence that must have been responsible for the destruction of the building. He assumed at first that an earthquake was responsible, but subsequent digging brought to light pumice, a volcanic substance. It was then that the idea occurred to him that what destroyed the villa, and in fact the palaces of Minoan Crete,

was not a mere earthquake but the eruption of the volcano of Santorini. The eruption would have created huge waves (tsunamis) which would not only have hit the coastal sites of Crete, but would undoubtedly have destroyed the fleet as well. In addition, hot ash would have burned the crops. The animals would not have been able to feed, and the whole economy would have collapsed. Sp. Marinatos proceeded to publish his theory "The volcanic destruction of Minoan Crete". At that time, in the 1930ies, very few people believed it was true. Thus, he made it his goal to go to Santorini someday and try to excavate there. If he found pottery of the same period as that of the destroyed palaces and villas in Crete, he would have a confirmation of his theory.

The excavations at Akrotiri

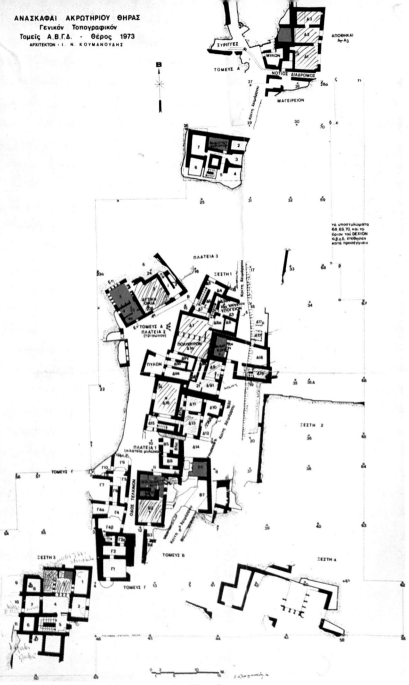

Plan of Akrotiri: The shrines are marked in red.

The room with the spring fresco.

Fresco, from the house of the Ladies.

The fresco of the river.

The fresco of the boxing children.

The stairway of the N. facade of sector D.

were very fruitful. What was discovered was a Minoan Pompey, the only well preserved settlement of the Bronze Age of about 1500 BC. The pottery found in the town is almost contemporary with that of Crete. So for many people the theory is vindicated, although not all are convinced. But the importance of the site is far greater than was expected even by the excavator. For the first time we have not only virtually intact walls and houses but whole frescoes, pottery on the places where it was left, furniture, even remnants of food. We can visualize and reconstruct the life of those people of the 16th century BC; we can also tell some things about their social organization and about their relationship with Crete.

The Earthquake and the Eruption

What we can infer from the archaeological evidence about the eruption is very interesting. We can tell that an earthquake preceeded the eruption of the volcano. Although we cannot know the exact time interval between the earthquake and the eruption we know that it must have been at least a year. Seeds, which were left on the ruins of the houses, had begun to germinate when the first ash fell. This means that the inhabitants had been forced to abandon their houses well before the volcano erupted. It explains why no skeletons of humans or animals (with the exception of a pig) have been found. What is more, people had the time to collect all

View of the magazines, sector A.

their valuables: jewelry, seal-stones, most bronzes, even tools. It is clear therefore, that not only did they have plenty of time at their disposal, but that they got well organized for a mass migration. We know that they left Akrotiri, but as of yet, we have no idea where they went. Perhaps we will find evidence of their colony somewhere on the mainland or Crete. The earthquake was very destructive. It is responsible for the ruinous state of the houses that you see on the site because once ash began falling from the volcano, the houses were packed so well, that they escaped any further damage in the centuries to come. But why did the people leave? Usually they stay to rebuild their stricken town. We do not know the answer, but we can speculate. Perhaps some smoke from the volcano warned them that worse was to come. Perhaps their priests had dreams of warning and forced them to leave, much as Moses led his people through the desert. It seems, however, that some people lingered on in the ruins even after the majority of the population had left. Sp. Marinatos called them troglodytes (dwellers in the ruins). Ch. Doumas, who is carrying on the excavations now, thinks they were a team repairing the ruined buildings. These people managed to escape as well, because we have not found their skeletons. But we can infer their presence because things were moved around **on the ash and volcanic pumice,** a certain testimony that some humans were present at the time of the eruption.

The cathedral at Pyrgos.

The village of Pyrgos.

Society and Religion

No written documents were
found at Akrotiri yet; conse-
quently our inferences about the
society have to be based on the
archaeological material. This
can be very revealing however.
First of all we can tell that Akrotiri was a very wealthy town.
Despite the systematic removal
of all the valuables, the quality of
the frescoes, the pottery and last
but not least the magnificence of
the buildings themselves testify
to an important community.
Several types of buildings can be
distinguished. Isolated houses
built with dressed ashlar stones,
isolated houses built with mud
brick, and blocks of dwellings.
Clearly the architecture reveals
something about the hierarchy of
the society. The isolated buildings would be the dwellings of
the more important officials. So
far no palace has been discovered, therefore there existed
no king. We must be cautious,
however, because the excavation
is far from being finished. In the
very south of the settlement, just
as the visitor enters, there must
have existed the religious and ad-
ministrative centre of the community. This can be deduced by
the importance of the buildings
most of them built in ashlar
masonry. It is impossible to tell

The fresco of the Marine Festival

how many people lived in each building. By analogy with other cultures, we can suppose that the masters slept and lived in the upper storeys while the servants or workers slept down below. It is likely that the quarters of the latter were much more cramped, and many people slept even in the storage-rooms among the jars.

An interesting point about the town is that we do not have industrial quarters, residential areas, suburbia, slums like in a modern city. Although there exists a concentration of industrial quarters on one area of the site (sector), in most cases, we have the following picture: upper storeys are residential and ceremonial quarters, while the ground floors and basements are industrial quarters. Thus, we have a vertical, not a horizontal division in society. This surely has implications for our understanding of the nature of the social hierarchy. I suggest that industry and economy were controlled **per building.** As we shall see, the masters of these buildings were not just wealthy people but officiated as priests as well.

What kind of industry did there exist in the ground floors of the buildings? The most important were mills where the grain was ground into flour and was distributed to the people. It is not an accident that one mill was situated at a square so that people could come and procure the amount of flour which was probably alotted to them as payment. A broad door and window

in the mill facilitated transactions.

We know that in Egypt, the pharaoh paid his subjects in kind for their services. It is very likely that the same was the case at Akrotiri.

Apart from mills, Akrotirians had metal work-shops, lapidary workshops for the making of stone objects, pottery workshops etc. Large storage areas or magazines existed as well, serving the needs of the community rather than single family units. Such is the case with the N. magazines of sector A and with room B1. The communal magazines imply that some form of collective economy was operative at Akrotiri; more will be said about that later.

Regarding the people's diet, we can infer the following on the basis of the food remnants that have been found. Beans, lentils, pulses, bread, sheep, goats, deer, pigs were the vegetables, plants and animals which were consumed.

Their furniture was quite elaborate. Beds, stools and a nice table have been reconstructed on the basis of casts which were made from imprints that these furniture made on the ash. Otherwise wooden objects do not survive, of course.

Domestic arrangements are also in evidence. A few kitchens have been identified by the presence of hearths and cooking pots. What is significant in this context, is that the kitchens in question do not appear to have belonged to a single household

but rather to a community of families. This can be deduced by the presence of several cooking pots and conical cups (which would have served as plates) in a single room. The cooking pots and cups are so numerous, that

View on the town of Phira.

one simply has to infer communal meals.

The subject of religion has been one of my main concerns. This is because religion is everywhere in evidence: in the pottery, in the frescoes, in the architecture. Very much of the pottery is cultic in character and we can identify it on the basis of Cretan equivalents. The most common type is a conical vase called **rhyton** which was used for

libations (liquid offerings to the deity). Another form of rhyton or libation vase has the form of an animal, a bull or a lion. The reason is that many animals were sacred to the gods and were often sacrificed to them. Other cultic equipment comprises tables of offerings, which are low tables on which one could place bloodless offerings to the divinity. This cultic equipment is found in many rooms at Akrotiri. Some of these rooms were simple storage areas or treasuries, but others were painted with frescoes. The latter rooms were undoubtedly shrines where rituals were performed. These shrines are always associated with industrial quarters

or with kitchens. For example there was a shrine above the storage room B1 and the kitchen room B2. There was also a shrine associated with one of the mills. This can mean one thing: the priests were in charge of the economic activities at Akrotiri and the society was theocratic (dominated and operated by

OIA

Panoramic view of the bay (Caldera).

religious institutions). Thus, the priests would have formed the elite, the aristocracy of society. They would have controlled trade and production. they would have amassed wealth which they would use for the embelishment of the town but also to pay the people who worked for them. The crafsmen, the artists, the scribes would all have had to be supported. The model which propose might sound strange to modern ears, but it was the accepted way of life in the contemporary civilizations of the Near East. There also, economy was controlled by the temple, if not by the King.

What kinds of gods did the Akrotirians worship? Here it is very difficult to give an answer. It is impossible to penetrate the minds of people who lived several thousands of years ago and to visualize their beliefs, if we have no written records. All we have is pictures, their frescoes. We also know that their religion was similar to that of contemporary Minoan Crete because the Cretans used the same type of cult equipment and painted the same types of frescoes. Looking at the religious evidence from both Akrotiri and Crete, we can deduce the following: A lot of the cult was related to fertility and vegetation. We can be sure of this because the frescoes often depict scenes of nature, while vegetation is the most frequent motif on their pottery. One type of pot, which must have been a cult vessel, deserves special attention because of its obvious connotations of fertility. It has an anthropomorphic shape, resembling a woman, with breasts, earrings and sometimes necklaces. Not infrequently, these types of pots which are called "Breasted ewers", have plant motifs painted on them. There can be no clearer indication of the associations of fertility with a female divinity. In fact, the Minoan goddess is often depicted on frescoes or on sealstones. She is also depicted on a fresco from Akrotiri, which is not yet published, and where she sits on a platform flanked by a griffin and a monkey. Were there any male gods? Here scholars disagree and some want to see a society dominated only by women. This is very unlikely, however. Male priests certainly existed as well, and it is hardly imaginable that male gods are completely absent in any religion. Thus, although Minoan and Akrotirian religion seems to put more emphasis on the goddess of fertility, male gods are not to be excluded. Animals were important for the religion of

Oia : The cathedral.

Because religion was, to a great extent, concerned with fertility, flowers played a great role in the lives of the Akrotirians. Lilies, crocuses, ivy and papyrus plants are frequently depicted on frescoes and on the pottery.

Judging from the architectural evidence, the Akrotirians had no detached temples of the form that we find in Egypt, the Near East or even later Greece.

these people. Monkeys and horned animals (bulls, deer, goats, antelopes) as well as lions were thought of as special companions of the gods. This is why they often feature on religious representations either together with the goddess or guarding her shrine. The animals also appear in the form of **rhyta** (offering vessels) which are very charming works of art as well as characteristic cult equipment).

The village of Perissa

Rather, they had small-scale shrines which were incorporated in buildings which served a variety of functions. Thus, we may assume that in a given building there existed a shrine, an industrial sector, magazines for storage and living quarters. Although the building was principally the residence of the priests, we cannot call it a temple because its principal function was not to house the cult image of the deity. According to historians of religion, we must use the word temple only if the cult, which took place there, was centered around the cult image of the god. But at Akrotiri we have found no traces of cult images. It is true that had they existed, the inhabitants would have carried them away. However, we have found no suitable architec-

tural arrangement such as a platform or a niche in which the presumed cult image would have stood.

To return to the shrines at Akrotiri. There were many, as I have already mentioned, corresponding to the number of buildings and blocks. They were all painted with frescoes. They were small, so that only a few priests could perform the required rituals in them. But was there no large place for public worship? Were the common people barred from cult? This of course is not the case. We know that public worship took place out in the open, in the fields, in caves, on top of the mountains.

Perissa beach

From Crete we have both pictorial and archaeological evidence to confirm this, and given the similarity between Akrotirian and Cretan (Minoan) religion, we have every reason to believe that the same was the case with Akrotiri. Thus, the shrines in the settlement served only as the focus of the religious administration. The priests performed the necessary rituals there, but they were also responsible for the economy and welfare of the community.

The shrines may have been associated with different festivals which were crucial for the entertainment of the people and which acted as cohesive forces in society, much as Christmas or Easter function for us. These festivals, to which the frescoes allude, included a harvest or spring festival, a marine festival, initiation festivals for the younger members of the community etc. Many of them, in fact almost all, took place outdoors with a large number of spectators watching.

The beach at Acrotiri (Red beach).

Picturesque beach

The village of Kamari

Relations with Crete

One of the interesting points which emerged from the excavations of Akrotiri, was the similarity of its art and architecture with Minoan Crete. Crete was at the peak of her culture at that time around 1500 B.C. She apears to have had a powerful fleet with which she dominated the sea, the so-called **Minoan Thalassocracy.** For this reason, some scholars supposed that Akrotiri was, in fact, a Minoan colony serving trade purposes. This is not the case however. Akrotiri was built many centuries before it became Minoanized, and many of its architectural features have a strong Cycladic flavour. It is clearly not a colony but a Cucladic town which is **strongly minoanized.** The pottery is imitating Minoan pottery, the great buildings copy Minoan

architectural features, the frescoes are painted in the Minoan tradition with Minoan subjects. Most of all, **the religion is Minoan.** All this requires an explanation. Could it be that the influence is only superficial? For

The village Phinikia and beyond, Oia.

example, Europe is very Americanized today if we judge from jeans, coca cola, hamburgers, American TV programmes and movies and many other items. Still, European culture has not merged with the American one, and certainly Europe is not militarily dominated by the USA. Some scholars think that this is the case with Akrotiri. Minoan influence does not mean domination but simply a cultural influence. But

this does not explain why Minoan religion was taken over. I believe that the Minoans brought Santorini into their sphere of influence **through religion itself.** Was that not what the Jesuits did in China and Japan in the 16th century? By proselytizing these people into Christianity they were able to build a formidable economic empire. In conclusion, Akrotiri was under the sphere of influence of Crete, an influence that was exerted through religion. It was not a Minoan colony, however.

The Frescoes

Most of the Akrotiri frescoes are on exhibit in the National Museum in Athens. They all depict scenes of a religious content although this is hard for the modern spectator to understand. But art in this period was functional, it served a purpose. It expressed the official ideology of the society, an ideology which was either political or religious or a mixture of both. In this case we have no political propaganda as in Egypt where the person of the pharaoh is depicted in many places and in many forms, we have only religious art.

Fresco of the Ladies. These are only two fragments from a larger composition which depicted a series of ladies, dressed in elaborate dresses and wearing earrings and other jewelry. They were most probably carrying gifts to a seated goddess(?) or a shrine. In the background of these ladies, there were papyrus plants, which are sacred plants to the divinity.

Fresco of Papyrus Plants. This is from the same composition as the ladies mentioned above. Papyrus plants grow in Egypt and were taken over by the Minoans and Akrotirians from there. They are most probably sacred like the lilies and crocuses.

Spring Fresco with Lilies. The painting depicts lilies growing in a rocky landscape. The colours are almost an impressionistic rendering of light reflected on the rocks. The red and brown rocks are reminiscent of the Akrotiri landscape of today. The lilies, growing from these rocks are not static. The Minoan artist avoided monotony at all costs, so he made them bend slightly, thus giving the impression of a breeze. The lily flowers are depicted in all the phases of their life: buds, just opening flowers, and fully

The village of Episkopi Gonia.

returning from an expedition, another interpretation commemorated a victory of the Therans over their enemy. The procession of ships celebrates this victory in a festival which is a thanks-giving

The crater of volcano.

opened flowers. Swallows are courting in the air. This animates the painting and, at the same time, tells you what it is all about: the coming of the Spring.

The Ship fresco. This was part of a frieze which was set above the windows of room **5** in the "West House". It depicts a fleet returning to a home port. Although the excavator originally assumed that the fleet was

to the deity. The religious character of the procession can be
deduced from the special adorn-
ments of the ships especially the
leading one (to the right of the
picture). It should be noted that
crocus flowers hang from the fes-
toons. Also the ships are not ro-
wed but paddled, an impractical
method if the journey is to be
imagined as a long one. Most
probably it was only a short trip

Picturesque chapel on the Road to Oia.

from one island town to Akrotiri itself. The military character can be deduced from the presence of helmets and spears which hang from the cabins of the captains of the ships. Finally the lions, which are emblems on the sides of some ships, definitely denote aggression. In this context one should note also the lion chasing a deer on the left of the picture, the purpose of which is to reinforce the theme of aggression.

The Tropical Landscape. It is a frieze which run across the E wall of room **5** of the West House. It should be understood in connection with the ship procession fresco above. It depicts two predatory animals an imaginary one, a griffin (lion with eagle's head) and a wild cat hunting near a river. The palms suggest a tropical landscape, and some have thought that it depicts a concrete place in Libya or the East. However, the presence of the imaginary animal, the griffin, suggests that this is only a genre scene, the purpose of which is to show **aggression.** As we have seen hunting is present also in the ship fresco symbolized by the lion emblems of the ships as well as the hunting lion on the landscape to the upper left of the ship fresco. Thus, the two friezes together allude to hunting and aggression.

The Fisherman. There were in fact two very similar frescoes of "fishermen" set in two corners of the same room where the ship fresco was found. The fish establish a thematic link with the marine festival of the ship fresco. Although the men are usually called fishermen, they are special servants of the deity. This can be argued because of two special features which characterize them: their partially shaved head and their nudity. Minoan males are never shown in the nude unless in the act of adoration: the god had to see you in all your purity. Therefore, the frescoes depict two adorants who are in the act of offering fish. An offering table depicting fish, has been found in the corner where the adorants would meet, if they walked.

The Priestess. Found in room 4 of the West House the woman is undoubtedly a priestess because of her unusual attire. She is wearing a kind of sari, and on her head she has a tight-fitting blue cap on which a snake is sewn. The snake could have been made of cloth or leather. Snakes on headdresses of priestesses or goddesses are well known from

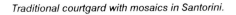

Traditional courtgard with mosaics in Santorini.

Crete. She is holding a vase with a long handle of a type that is attested archaeologically. It is not certain what was contained in it. Some have said there were burning coals, others cakes. I wonder if it is not red pigment which she has just applied on herself. Note her vivid red lips and red-painted ear which is surely a ritual adornment. It is interesting that red pigment in a broken bowl was found in the room of the priestess.

The Cabin-Screen Fresco. It was found in room **4** of the West House next to room **5** of the adorant fishermen and the ship fresco. It cannot be understood out of context because it depicts the cabin-screen of the leader of the fleet of the ship fresco. Here you see only one example; in reality, there were found seven to eight of these frescoes all depicting similar, but not identical, cabin-screens. This has a special significance, namely it connects the room, in which the fresco was found, with the leader of the fleet. Sp. Marinatos thought that

this was the admiral's room, but since the ship-fresco shows a religious procession with a military character, the leader of the fleet must have had some religious function as well. Indeed this is shown by the stylized lilies which adorn the top of the poles. It will be remembered that lilies are sacred flowers to the divinity. We must imagine the cabins as made

Oia built on the edge of the cliff

124

of animal hides attached to wooden poles.

The Monkeys. The composition is, to a large extent, restored out of incomplete fragments, but the subject is clear: monkeys climbing on rocks in an animated fashion. The rocks are rendered schematically, but the monkeys are very life-like. This is the strength of the Minoan painters that they render such convincing pictures of nature, especially animals. What the rest of the composition depicted, we do not know, but monkeys are often shown as special servants of the deity. On an unpublished fresco from Akrotiri, a monkey touches the goddess, whereas on another he is shown in front of an altar.

White and blue are the dominating colours in Santorini.

Coutemporary architecture at Oia.

The Antelopes. We see here only one pair of antelopes which are so realistically rendered, that we can identify the species: Oryx Beissa. There were actually six antelopes painted in the room, two pairs and two single ones. They are painted in simple outline but with a marvelously convincing effect. They are probably not courting as was originally suggested. They seem to belong to the same sex because they have the same size. I believe they

are engaged in playful competition as young animals are prone to do in the spring. The ivy border above them also suggests spring-time activity.

The Boxing Children. They

come from the same room as the antelopes and there is a thematic link between these compositions. The children are engaged in playful activity and competition just as the antelopes are. They are not ordinary children but special servants of the deity because they have partially shaved heads. One of them wears also jewelry, earrings, a necklace and bracelets. Given the fact that athletic contests were always connected with some religious festival in antiquity (like the Olympic games of Classical Greece were performed in the honour of Zeus), it is a religious festival that is depicted here. The mood is cheerful and a kind of **joie de vivre** dominates both compositions.

The Pottery and Other Vessels

Of the hundreds of pots that have been discovered at Akrotiri, some characteristic samples only are available for the visitor. One can divide the pottery and other vessels in the following categories: **Bronze Jugs and pans.** These are rare because most were taken away by the inhabitants, but what remains gives us a glimpse of the high technology of the Aegean bronze smiths.

Phira : The bay and beyond the island of N. kameni (Volkano).

View of the island Nea Kameni (Volcano)

Cook-ware: These are usually coarse pottery and comprise cooking pots, ovens and stands for spits.

Grinding vessels and Mortars. They are made of stone and represent the most ordinary, low quality vessels that you find in Akrotiri. They were used for grinding and pounding various substances ranging from corn to pigments.

Jugs. The majority of the vases are jugs painted mostly with floral motifs although some have birds. The floral motifs are copied from Cretan pottery and are connected with the idea of fertility and vegetation which we meet constantly in Minoan and

Akrotirian art. A special category are the **nippled ewers** which allude to fertility and the female goddess. Many of the jugs are imported from Crete as we can tell from their lustrous surface. Nippled ewers, however, represent a local tradition and they are always locally made.

Flower pots. Some vases appear to have had no practical function, and they seem to have been constructed solely for the purpose of holding flowers.

Tables of Offering. Tripod low tables of circular form have been found in some numbers at Akrotiri. They are found in shrines. Two of such a type were found in the West House together with the frescoes, all of which allude to a marine festival.

The small harbour at the Volcano

Pithoi or Storage Jars. They vary in size and decoration, but were all used for storage of liquids and other substances such as flour, honey etc.

Guide to the Antiquities

The first building you see to your left, as you approach the site and before your ticket is checked, is **XESTE 3.** It is one of the most grandiose buildings of the site built with ashlar masonry (dressed blocks) in its facade. It was used for ceremonial purposes because it contains many large rooms. The frescoes revolve around themes of vegetation, animals and the goddess. It

included domestic or service rooms which are much smaller in size and which contained tools and storage jars. To the S. of the building you will note stone tools lying around. These belong to the people that were left behind after the destructive earthquake but before the eruption (see above, "The Earthquake and the Eruption"). They were obviously planning to repair the building but they never got that far.

After having entered the roofed area, you are walking on a street which runs N-S through the settlement. To the left you have **Sector Γ**. The industrial installations of the town are most evident there, although they are present in virtually every building. You will note many stone tools lying around, as well as troughs and mortars. In these rooms workers pounded and worked various substances and possibly repaired damages, as can be deduced from the presence of hammers and anvils.

To your right is **Sector B.** Note the small windows on the level of the street which gave access to light into the basement and workshops of this sector. Tree-trunks were inserted in the walls (now restored with gypsum) to give them more elasticity and render them earthquake resistant. As you proceed

The plain of Oia when many of the products of the islands are grown.

The village of Pyrgos and beyond, Phira.

The village of Vothonas.

northwards, you will reach a small square. Facing you is a mill. The bench on which the miller sat, and the clay bucket in which he poured the flour, are still in situ. Through the large door of the mill, distribution of flour would take place to the people gathered in the square. Across from the mill and to the south is room B1 of sector B. It is the room of the **Antelopes and Boxing Children,** and it was a shrine because it contained a small treasury with cultic equipment. Note the large window facing the square where the priests could have appeared for the public to see. Thus the square serves a double purpose, one secular (flour distribution) and one religious.

Moving on to the North, you will reach another square larger than the first. This is dominated by the **West House.** It has irregular windows because symmetry was not striclty observed, nor was it such an important aesthetic ideal as later. Its most interesting feature is the large window. I believe it was a window of appearances as the previous one of B1. Indeed the fresco of the priestess, the adorants carrying fish as well as the ship fresco frieze were found in this building. We may imagine that the priestess appeared from the window to the people below. The West House was evidently a "cult centre" with a shrine above and industrial quarters below. A kitchen, a metallurgy workshop, grinding stones and storage jars were found in the groundfloor. Here economy and religion are combined in a characteristic manner.

While you are in the square, you can look through the windows of **sector D,** which is to your right as you are facing the West House. You will see a typical basement with storage jars and other pottery. Some pieces of

Oia and the island of Therassia with background.

furniture, including a table were recovered from there. If you continue to the North, you will pass the **"House of the Ladies"** on your left. There, the frescoes with the Ladies and the Papyruses were found. It contained also rich store-rooms and a lapidary's workshop: an unfinished marble vase was found in this building.

The most Northern building **Sector A** is a big store-room. It had three rooms in a row, containing many storage jars and big

View from Imerovigli.

On the beach of Acrotiri, in a cav‹
is the taverna of Nicholas.

Imerovigli: picturesque lane.

windows for distribution purposes. Thus, it was a communal magazine. Next to it was a mill, whereas on the upper storey, there existed another shrine.

Now you start going South, to look at the **region East of the street.** You will be looking at **sectors D and B** from the other side. Note that these are blocks, not isolated buildings. Each unit had a shrine. Room D2 was the shrine of the Lilies where the fresco with the same name was found.

There was also the shrine of the Antelopes and Boxing Children, mentioned above, and the shrine with the Monkey fresco. Industrial quarters, kitchens, mills and storage areas are distributed in these sectors, and they are always close to shrines. A millstone was found next to the Lilies shrine, a storage room was below the Antelope and Boxing children shrine etc. Note the impressive Eastern facade of sector D standing three storeys high.